THE 3 THINGS THAT WILL
CHANGE YOUR DESTINY TODAY!

For more information on Paul McKenna and his books,
see his website at www.paulmckenna.com

www.**transworldbooks**.co.uk

THE 3 THINGS THAT WILL CHANGE YOUR DESTINY TODAY!

•

PAUL MCKENNA PH.D.

EDITED BY MICHAEL NEILL

BANTAM PRESS

LONDON · TORONTO · SYDNEY · AUCKLAND · JOHANNESBURG

TRANSWORLD PUBLISHERS
61–63 Uxbridge Road, London W5 5SA
www.transworldbooks.co.uk

Transworld is part of the Penguin Random House group of companies
whose addresses can be found at global.penguinrandomhouse.com

First published in Great Britain in 2015 by Bantam Press
an imprint of Transworld Publishers

A CIP catalogue record for this book
is available from the British Library.

ISBN 9780593064030

Typeset in 11/16pt Palatino by Julia Lloyd Design
Printed and bound by Clays Ltd, Bungay, Suffolk

Penguin Random House is committed to a sustainable
future for our business, our readers and our planet. This book
is made from Forest Stewardship Council® certified paper.

1 3 5 7 9 10 8 6 4 2

For Kate, the love of my life!

A QUICK NOTE FROM PAUL

Congratulations – today is the day you are going to change your destiny!

In just a few hours, the direction of your whole life will change for the better. These changes have become possible because of some astounding breakthroughs in science, psychology and spirituality that I will be sharing with you in this book.

I'm sometimes a little cautious to make such dramatic claims, even though I know they are true. I've been watching people's lives change before my eyes for over twenty years now, and I absolutely know that change not only can happen in a moment, it most often does.

It might be the moment you met a particular person and your world changed for the better. The moment your first child was born. The death of a loved one. A diagnosis of an illness or the confirmation of a cure. The moment you were down on your knees and your prayers were answered, or the moment you were lying in the gutter and you looked up and saw the stars.

Over the next few hours, we're going to be doing three things together which I've seen change people's lives again and again. Each of these three things is designed to create 'moments of destiny': those life-changing moments where everything is different afterwards from what it was before.

I'll be doing most of the work here, reprogramming your mind by guiding you through a series of exercises and hypnotic sessions on the enclosed DVD and CD or on the downloads, but I do need two things from you. The first is an open mind, and the second is a few hours of your time. Give me that inch of trust and together we'll create miles and miles of positive change in your world.

HOW IT ALL WORKS

I've always thought about the science of personal change as being like going to a really great restaurant – you don't expect to have to cook the food yourself. But while I'll be your chef for the next 24 hours, I am going to rely on you to provide the ingredients.

I'll be asking you to take stock of your life as I guide you through five simple techniques that will change your destiny for good. Doing these techniques won't take up much of your time – even the longest one should take no more than twenty minutes, and I'll guide you through them step by step on the video and audio that come with the book.

I've tested this system time and time again on hundreds of people from all walks of life, and it always works – *if* people follow my instructions. That's not to say you need to do it all perfectly. Nobody ever does. But you do need to *do* them in order to get the results you desire. And these techniques are so robust that even when people do them badly, they somehow still get to experience positive changes that make it all worthwhile.

My goal for you with this book is simple – tangible positive changes in every important area of your life. You will improve your health, relationships, career, finances and happiness. You will also begin to experience an overwhelming sense of optimism, a real heart-felt purpose, an expanded consciousness, and a sense of confidence and passion for the future.

You have nothing to lose and everything to gain. Shall we begin?

ABOUT THE DVD / CD / DOWNLOADS

This isn't just a book, it's an integrated life-change system. To get the most from the system, it's essential that you use the video and audio techniques as described. They are on the DVD and CD that come with the book and are also available as a series of downloads that can be saved directly to your computer, or streamed via your smartphone or tablet to watch and listen to whenever you want.

You can find the details on the special card at the front of the book. When you go to www.paulmckenna.com/downloads, you then simply enter your unique personal code from the card to access the video and audio techniques. Then you have me on tap 24 hours a day to help you with your positive life change.

To make the whole experience as easy as possible, as you read the book I will describe each technique we are going to do, and then you simply use the CD, DVD or download to do the life-changing technique, with me taking you through each step of the process.

GETTING STARTED

•

TAKING BACK
YOUR LIFE

*'It is not in the stars to hold our
destiny but in ourselves.'*
WILLIAM SHAKESPEARE

•

CHAPTER ONE

Are You Destined to Succeed?

Beating the odds

Palm readers believe that your left hand is what you are born with and your right hand tells the story of what you do with it. In other words, regardless of the hand you're dealt in life, it's always going to be up and down to you what you choose to do with it.

Just for fun, here's a list of famous people and the afflictions they were born with – see if you can identify which affliction goes with which person.

Sir Winston Churchill	Partially blind
Dame Agatha Christie	Partially deaf
Sir Isaac Newton	Asperger's syndrome
Ludwig von Beethoven	Speech impediment
Albert Einstein	Dyslexia

- **Sir Winston Churchill had a speech impediment, yet went on to become known as one of the greatest orators of the twentieth century.**

- **Dame Agatha Christie had all the symptoms of what is now known as dyslexia yet wrote more than 70 books that sold over 2 billion copies.**

- **Ludwig von Beethoven composed his ninth and final symphony, considered by many to be the greatest work in all classical music, while almost completely deaf.**

- **Sir Isaac Newton went partially blind as a young scientist yet recovered to develop the theory of gravity and the basis of both physics and calculus.**

- **Albert Einstein exhibited all the traits of the modern diagnosis of Asperger's syndrome, yet his theory of relativity revolutionized modern science and led to the development of nuclear energy.**

Given what they were up against, would you predict that each one of them would go on to greatness? Or would it seem like the difficulties they had to face in life meant they were destined to fail?

I was constantly told at school that I would never amount to anything in life. But I determined early on that I wasn't going to let someone else's diagnosis of my problems become a prognosis for how things would turn out in my life.

And the same thing is true for you. Like everybody else, you were born with a potential. You got all the genetic advantages of a human being, from a rational, creative brain to opposable thumbs. And yet if you're like most people, you're probably more aware of what you don't have than what you do.

Did you have a difficult childhood? So did Oprah Winfrey, Kevin Spacey, Charlize Theron and over 50 per cent of the most successful men and women in the world.

Do you have learning difficulties? So did Thomas Edison, Richard Branson, Alexander Graham Bell, Hans Christian Andersen and George Washington.

Have you been serially unemployed, completely broke, fired from your job or even bankrupt? So were Bill Gates, Simon Cowell, Lady Gaga, Jay Z and millions of others.

If there's one thing that life has taught me, it's that it isn't what you're born with or what happens to you in life – it's the choices you make along the way that determine your ultimate destiny. Choice is power, and it's a power you will be identifying, developing and working with throughout our time together.

The science of possibility

In the past 50 years or so, scientists have begun to explore the impact of attitude and belief on the physical body. In one of the most interesting sets of experiments I have come across, the late Dr Masaru Emoto took twice distilled or 'pure' water and exposed it to four sets of stimuli – words, pictures, music and prayer. He then froze the water and photographed the crystals that formed afterwards.

For example, he took one jar of water and wrote the words 'Thank you' on it. He then took another jar of water and wrote the words 'You fool' on it.

He froze each jar and did an analysis of the water crystals under a microscope. Here's what he discovered:

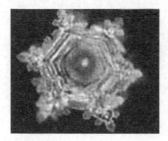 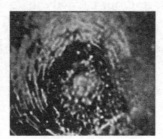

Thank you (Chinese)   You fool (Japanese)

The results were consistent – when the water was exposed to positive words, images, music and prayer, the crystals were beautiful, unique and symmetrical; when the opposite stimuli were given, the crystals were either disfigured or didn't form at all.

Now, if you think about it, human beings are over 60 per cent water. The implications for the impact of our own internal thoughts and images on the body are staggering. What we think about all day long is literally shaping our physical destiny, day by day and moment by moment.

In the late 1970s, a new field in medicine emerged, known as psychoneuroimmunology, or PNI, studying the impact of our psychology on our physiology – what is more commonly known as the mind–body connection. One of the early researchers in the field, a neuropharmacologist named Candace Pert, discovered that the body is hard-wired with links between our immune system and our emotions. More recent studies have shown undeniable links between our thoughts, the stress response, and both our susceptibility to illness and our capacity to heal. It seems that the more closely we study the body, the more we discover about the direct connection between how we think and how we feel.

The power of hypnosis for change

In his fun and inspiring TEDx talk, my longtime friend and world-renowned life coach Michael Neill asks his audience, 'Why aren't we awesomer?' He goes on to demonstrate how we are all held back by the limits of our own perception.

One of the drawings he shares in the talk to illustrate his point is an optical illusion known as the Kanizsa triangle:

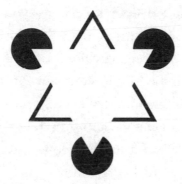

Nearly everyone who looks at this image can clearly see a bold, white, upside-down triangle connecting and overlapping an equilateral black triangle and three black dots in the picture. Yet the truth is, there are no complete triangles (or in fact dots) in the picture.

Our minds fill in the lines to create what we expect to see in our imaginations. In the same way, our perceptions and expectations from the past cause us to see the world in a certain way, even if what we see only exists inside our mind.

In my own career, I have seen people who used to think of themselves as not very bright score at genius level on exams. A woman who had been paralysed as a result of an emotional trauma got up and walked, and a man who had been functionally blind for over seven years began to see, simply through changing their perceptions and expectations and tapping into the power of the mind.

In this book and on the accompanying DVD, CD and downloads, I will be using hypnosis to help you tap into your potential at a deeper level than you may ever have thought possible. In addition, we will be using cutting-edge techniques and a new science called 'Havening' to change the structure of your brain to shift your perceptions and open you up to possibilities that may not even be on your radar yet.

But in order for me to help you, there is one thing you need to do first. This is a strange request, so I encourage you not to say 'yes' too quickly:

Are you willing to be wrong?

Would it be OK with you if it turns out that you are more powerful than you suspect, more capable than you know and more creative than you have ever noticed?

Here are a few things to reflect on as you consider your answer:

- **It isn't what you're born with or what happens to you in life, it's the choices you make along the way that determine your ultimate destiny.**

- **Choice is power.**

- **There is a direct and undeniable link between how we think and how we feel.**

- **Our perceptions and expectations from the past cause us to see the world in a certain way, even if what we see only exists inside our mind.**

CHAPTER TWO

•

Taking Your Life Back

You are not a victim

When I hypnotize someone on stage to do extraordinary things, most people think that I am taking a person who is wide awake and putting them into a trance. But the truth is, we all walk around in various stages of trance all day long. Think about zoning out on a long car journey or train ride. Suddenly you find yourself at your destination with little or no memory of how you got there. Or in an lift, watching the floor numbers go up and down without any sense of the people around you.

One of the most common trances that people walk around in is the 'victim trance' – the misapprehension that they are victims of the world around them and have no choice but to respond in fixed ways to whatever it is that happens in their life. My friend the late author Robert Anton Wilson used to describe these limited perceptions as reality tunnels, because they give us a kind of tunnel vision that only allows us to see evidence of what we already think and believe. Wilson called this phenomenon Orr's Law – the idea that whatever the thinker thinks, the prover proves.

What that means is that your ideas about yourself and what's possible for you are not fixed or solid. You have learned to believe in your limitations, and have unwittingly used Orr's Law to gather evidence to 'prove' their existence. But these ideas and perceptions are not really yours, they're learned – stray ideas and random thoughts you've picked up along the way. And the good news is that anything you've learned can be unlearned.

For example, far too many people I've met sit around and blame their lives on the world around them. They complain about everyone and everything, from their parents to the economy and their health to the state of the environment.

And these people do have a point. Life isn't always fair, and it certainly isn't always easy. Bad things do sometimes happen to good people, and I've never met anyone who hasn't been let down or ripped off at least once in their lives. But the difference between those people who thrive in spite of their circumstances and the ones who seem doomed to be thrown around at the mercy of their environment is a simple one. The people who struggle are lost in a trance, seeing themselves as victims of a system set up to benefit other people at the cost of themselves. The ones who thrive have woken up to the fact that we make our own choices in life, and that it is the sum total of those choices that creates our destiny.

For example, in 2008 I sat down to interview the billionaire Philip Green as part of the research for my book *I Can Make You Rich*. He told me the story of how at one point early in his career his fortune had been taken from him in a business deal and years of hard work were wiped out overnight. One day he was a multi-millionaire; the next he was worth £20,000.

When I asked him how he had handled it, he told me, 'I picked myself up, I dusted myself off, and I bet on my own judgement. I took half the money we had left and booked my wife and I on a holiday at an exclusive resort in the Caribbean. We spent the week relaxing, enjoying each other's company and imagining the future we would like to create.'

Since that island getaway, Philip has become known as 'the high street billionaire' and one of the world's leading philanthropists. What allowed him to turn his personal misfortune into a global fortune? Something that nearly every happy and successful person I have ever met has at an almost unconscious level: a recognition of the built-in human capacity for resilience – to bounce back from any life circumstance and come back with even more resourcefulness than they had before.

The Christmas ornament, the orange and the rubber ball

In his wonderful book on resilience, *Bounce: The Art of Turning Tough Times into Triumph*, bestselling author Keith McFarland shares an analogy for the three ways that companies respond to difficulties in their lives: Christmas ornaments, oranges and rubber balls. If we are like a Christmas ornament, we do what it takes to look good on the surface, but we see ourselves as fundamentally fragile and easy to break. If we are like an orange, we have a tough skin but every time something goes wrong we get a little more bruised until eventually we begin to rot away from the inside. If we are like a rubber ball, we have no fear of being dropped on our heads or of things going wrong in our life. Quite simply, we were made to bounce.

In my work with high achievers, I see this 'rubber ball' quality at play all the time. No matter what life seems to throw at them and how hard they get knocked down, they seem to be able to get back up with more 'bounce' in their step than before. Fortunately, this quality is not something that some people are born with and others aren't. It's inside all of us – and it can be brought to the surface through a bit of subconscious reprogramming and a recognition of the power of choice.

There are a lot of people who see their experience of life as something that happens to them. So if it's a grey day, they feel bad; if it's a sunny day, they feel good. When things go the way that they want, they feel good; when things don't, they feel bad. If you were to observe them from a distance, it would seem as though there was a direct cause-and-effect relationship between the weather and their moods, or between how things turn out and the way that they feel.

That's a 'Christmas ornament' view of life – the idea that it's not we who make our way in the world, it's what happens to us. But not everyone feels bad when it rains and not everybody feels good when the sun shines. Not everyone wants to kill the traffic warden when they get a ticket and not everyone feels grateful when they get a gift. The difference that makes the difference is what Holocaust survivor Viktor Frankl called 'the last of the human freedoms – to choose one's attitude in any given set of circumstances, to choose one's own way'.

To better understand this, imagine you have an infinite number of pairs of glasses, each one with a special filter in the lens that will cause you to see the world in a certain light. When viewed through 'Christmas ornament' glasses, the world is filled with potential threats – things that could go wrong and cause you to 'break'. When viewed through 'orange' glasses, the world is tough and your job is to be tougher – to develop a thick skin and a tough outer layer of attitude that will keep the world at a distance and keep you safe even as you get battered and bruised by life.

But imagine for a moment that you put your 'rubber ball' glasses on. Suddenly, the world is a playground you can throw yourself into with abandon, because everything you bump into helps move you in a new direction. Every time you hit bottom it's simply another opportunity to bounce.

Now, in each of the three scenarios, the circumstances haven't changed. The circumstances are as they are, but the way we perceive things completely changes our experience.

So if it looks to you like you're being 'realistic' when you tell the story of how you're a victim of your circumstances, know that 'reality' is just a question of perception, and it changes according to what we think we are going to see. In science, this is called the 'observer effect'. Simply stated, the observer nearly always has an effect on the thing that is being observed in the experiment. So, for example, if you put a thermometer in your mouth to take your temperature, the presence of the thermometer actually changes the internal temperature of your body ever so slightly.

Now, in most things in nature, the impact of the observer on the observed is of minor consequence. But when it comes to our personal worldview, it's the most powerful thing in the world. And understanding this is the key to taking charge of your destiny:

The way we look at the world determines what we see.
Even a tiny change in the way you look at life
changes everything.

In the next chapter, I'll be asking you a series of questions about your life – where you've been, where you are and where you're headed. But, for now, just take a few moments to contemplate these key points:

- **The 'victim trance' is one of the most common delusions that people walk around with – you could say, that people are asleep to – in their lives.**

- **We can wake up from this trance in any moment. No matter what has happened to you up until this point in your life, you will always have choices about how you move forward.**

- **It's possible to live life as a Christmas ornament, an orange or a rubber ball. It's just a matter of perception.**

- **You have much more freedom than you think.**

CHAPTER THREE

•

A Snapshot in Time

Mapping your destiny path

One of the most unusual things about the work I do with clients is that the changes they undergo are often so dramatic they can't remember what it was like before the changes happened. This is because once the brain re-codes the way it thinks about a particular problem or situation for the better, there's no way back to the original.

So someone might come in with a phobia of spiders, but in less than an hour that lifelong phobia is gone and they can't imagine how they could ever have been afraid. They may even say something like, 'I guess I wasn't really phobic after all – sorry for wasting your time!' In fact, my friend and mentor Dr Richard Bandler used to run into this so often that he would jokingly suggest he could easily 'reinstall' the phobia if his client wanted to feel the terror again. That way they would know they had been cured!

So, in this chapter, before we begin with the cure, we want to take a kind of a mental snapshot of the problem. I'm going to ask you to take a look at your life at three different stages – how it is now, how it was in the past and how the amazing bio-computer between your ears predicts it will be in the future.

This will serve two purposes. First, it will give you some perspective on where you've been, where you are and where you're headed on your current life trajectory. Second, it will serve as the 'before' photograph for comparison after you've completed working through all the exercises in the book, watched all the videos and listened to the hypnotic trance. You'll be able to see how far you've come in just one day, and you'll be able to return to the circle again and again to see how much your destiny has changed over time.

I call the exercise we're about to do 'The Circle of Life'. It's incredibly simple, but please don't underestimate its power. If you take the time to answer the questions honestly and fill in the wheel, I guarantee you'll be surprised by how much you'll learn in the process.

What we're going to do is take a look at the six main areas of your life – your health, relationships, career, finances, happiness, and sense of larger meaning and purpose. For each of those areas, you're going to rate yourself on a scale from 1 to 10 where 1 is the lowest and 10 is as good as you can imagine things being. One of the reasons this exercise will give you such a powerful perspective on your life is because you are going to do this from three different points of view – how things look to you today, how they looked to you ten years ago, and how you suspect they'll look to you ten years from now if you continue on the destiny path you're currently on.

Here's a bit more about each of the six life areas we'll be exploring. After you've read through this section, I'll provide an easy visual version of the exercise so you can go through it in detail for yourself.

1. Health

Everyone thinks about health a little bit differently, but true health is more than just the absence of illness. It's a measure of the positive energy that's flowing through your system – what Oriental medicine often refers to as 'Chi', or what we in the West would typically call 'the life force' or 'vitality'.

When you give yourself a score for your health, be sure to take into account not only what a Western doctor might measure (weight, blood pressure, cholesterol, illness, etc.) but also your sense of vitality and aliveness.

2. Relationships

The quality of your relationships with others are one of the most important measuring sticks for the quality of your life. This includes your relationships with family, friends and significant others at home and at work.

If you have very different relationships with different people (i.e. a great relationship with your parents but a difficult relationship with your children, or a wonderful relationship with men but difficult relationships with women), give yourself a number based on how much you enjoy the people you spend the majority of your life with.

3. Career

Everybody does something to make their way in the world. Whether you're unemployed, a homemaker or a CEO, you spend a certain amount of time supporting yourself and others in the world.

Remember as you score yourself in this category that what matters is not what someone else would think of what you're up to in the world – it's the extent to which what you do is interesting, enjoyable and fulfilling *to you*.

4. Finances

Money is one of the most emotive things in the world – people tend to love it or hate it, and the pursuit of it (or dealing with an absence of it) seems to occupy an incredible amount of nearly everyone's time.

The score you give yourself for finances should not be a measure of how much you currently make or how much you have in the bank. Instead, give yourself a higher score if you feel a sense of ease, abundance and being supported by money, and a lower score if you feel a sense of stress, lack and hardship.

5. Happiness

Having spent many years researching happiness alongside many of the experts in the field and even writing a book on it, the one thing I can say definitively is that happiness is a natural human state, like hunger, anger, excitement, boredom, neutrality and alertness.

When you give yourself a number for happiness, look beyond your mood of the moment to your general sense of well-being. While we all have moments of sadness and moments of elation, what feels normal to you? What is your apparent 'happiness set point'?

6. Sense of larger meaning and purpose

One of the hidden dimensions of life is our connection to the larger whole – our relationship to the fact that we are part of something bigger than ourselves. If you are religious, you might think of this larger whole as 'God'; if you are spiritual but not religious, you might call it 'universal mind', 'the miracle of nature' or 'the human spirit'. Even people who don't believe in any outside agency beyond the human mind find meaning in committing themselves to some kind of a purpose beyond their own individual survival.

For better or for worse, however you think of whatever that larger whole is that you and your life are a part of, the number you give yourself in this category should be a reflection of your relationship with it.

Putting pen to paper

On the next page, you will find a blank circle of life for you to fill in. If you are reading this book on an electronic device, you can download a copy to print off at www.paulmckenna.com/downloads. Of course, you can also simply copy the drawing on to a piece of paper (or even a napkin) and fill it out there.

In order to assist you in completing this exercise, here are a few questions to help you:

The present
What year is it now? _____
What is your age? _____

The past
What year was it ten years ago? _____
What age were you then? _____

The future
What year will it be ten years from now? _____
What age will you be then? _____

Some people like to take each life area and look at it from all three time perspectives before moving on to the next; others prefer to go through all six life areas from the perspective of the present before repeating the process from the past and then again from the future.

However you do it, the process should take you between 5 and 15 minutes. *It is essential that you actually mark down your scores on paper and connect the dots to make a circle (or whatever shape they make).* Trying to do this in your head or skipping it altogether will be a waste of your time and will limit the value you get from the rest of this book.

Do it now!

THE CIRCLE OF LIFE

- On a scale from 1 to 10, how would you rate your **health**? How would you have rated it ten years ago? If you continue on the path you're on, how do you suspect you'll rate it ten years from now?

- On a scale from 1 to 10, how would you rate your **relationships**? How would you have rated them ten years ago? If you continue on the path you're on, how do you suspect you'll rate them ten years from now?

- On a scale from 1 to 10, how would you rate your **career**? How would you have rated it ten years ago? If you continue on the path you're on, how do you suspect you'll rate it ten years from now?

- On a scale from 1 to 10, how would you rate your **finances**? How would you have rated them ten years ago? If you continue on the path you're on, how do you suspect you'll rate them ten years from now?

- On a scale from 1 to 10, how would you rate your **happiness**? How would you have rated it ten years ago? If you continue on the path you're on, how do you suspect you'll rate it ten years from now?

- On a scale from 1 to 10, how would you rate your **sense of larger meaning and purpose**? How would you have rated it ten years ago? If you continue on the path you're on, how do you suspect you'll rate it ten years from now?

THE PAST

What year was it ten years ago? _____

What age were you then? _____

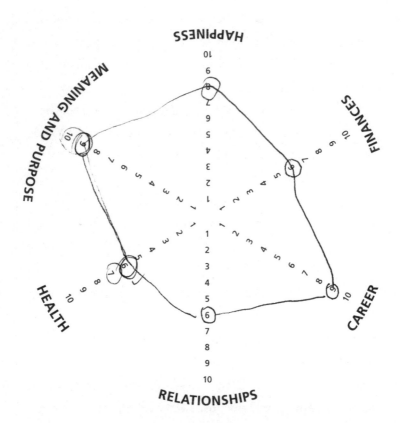

THE PRESENT

What year is it now? _____

What is your age? _____

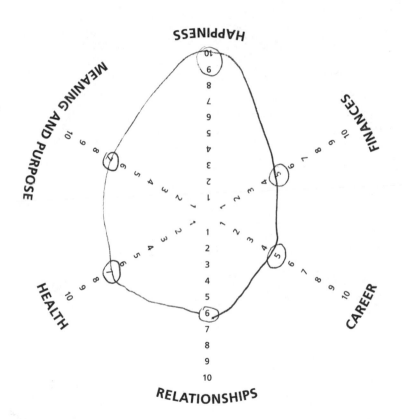

THE FUTURE

What year will it be ten years from now? _____

What age will you be then? _____

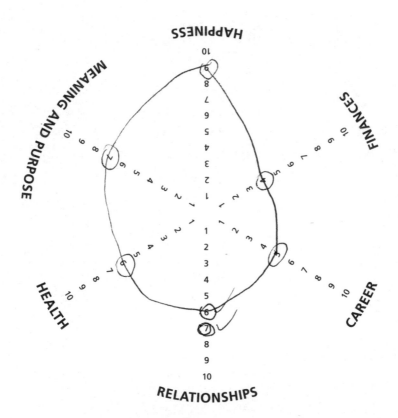

So, what does it all mean?

Having done this exercise many times, I know that people often wonder what to make of their results. Is it better to have higher numbers in some categories and lower in others (like a flat tyre), or uniformly even numbers that make a perfect circle even if the numbers are low?

Fortunately, **there are no right answers to these questions!** This exercise is simply a snapshot in time – a chance for you to get a visual perspective on where you are now, where you've come from and where you're headed. At the end of the book, after you've read through the text, done all the techniques at least once and listened to the hypnotic trance, I'll ask you to repeat this exercise and you'll be able to see how the shape of your life now (and your future destiny) has changed.

In the meantime, here are a few things to remember before moving forward to the first of the three things:

- **Before making a change, it's useful to get a clear picture of where you are now.**

- **Health is more than just the absence of illness.**

- **Absolutely everyone can be happy.**

IMPORTANT!

The most important thing in this book is to *actually do each and every one of the exercises*. Reading the book without doing the exercises is like reading a menu without eating the meal – it might be enjoyable but it won't be fulfilling. I have designed this system so that the book and techniques work together to change your destiny – you must do every exercise at least once and read the book all the way through to get the full benefit and have your world change significantly for the better!

THE FIRST THING

•

CLEARING
THE PAST

*'It is never too late to be what
you might have been.'*

GEORGE ELIOT

CHAPTER FOUR

•

The 'Magic Bullet'

In search of the secret to change

When I first got involved in the world of personal development, I was convinced that hypnosis was the 'magic bullet' that could take care of pretty much every problem known to man. I hypnotized everyone whether they liked it or not and essentially asked their subconscious mind to do whatever it needed to do to solve their problem or help them reach their goal. And surprisingly often, it worked.

So I learned more about the mind and began studying and then working alongside Dr Richard Bandler, the co-creator of NLP (Neuro-Linguistic Programming). Now, by learning about how the mind created and maintained problem states, I could target issues with specific algorithms designed to get straight to the heart of the matter. I shared these tools and techniques with everyone I could – over 100,000 people on live seminars and millions more through my books and CDs – but there were still some things that seemed difficult to reach with mind-programming techniques alone.

More experiments in more fields followed, with my time learning and working with TFT (Thought Field Therapy) among the most productive. I went to study with the late Dr Roger Callahan, creator of the field, and found the potential of his work extremely exciting.

But unbeknown to me, another man, Dr Ronald Ruden, was working equally hard to find his own version of a 'magic bullet' for change. Dr Ruden is that rarest of all things – a conventional medical doctor with an open mind, a background in neuroscience and a PhD in neuropharmacology, which is essentially the study of brain chemistry. He runs New York City's largest independent medical practice as a board certified and licensed internist – a specialization that is sometimes called 'the doctor's doctor'.

In his never-ending quest to help his patients, he too had come across TFT, and he was interested by the results it was able to produce with his patients, particularly those suffering from traumatic imprints. But he was also frustrated by the fact that, despite its effectiveness, the science behind it needed more research for it to be taken seriously by the medical profession.

So he initiated his own seven-year study, using brain scans to measure the specific impact of the different TFT, EMDR (Eye Movement Desensitization and Reprocessing) and other psycho-sensory protocols in creating change. ('Psycho-sensory' is a term used to describe any therapy that combines psychological techniques with physical touch or movement to produce change.) To his surprise, he found that while a few of the traditional moves used as a part of the conventional models did indeed have an impact on brain activity, a large portion of them were completely benign, doing neither harm nor good.

Excited at the possibilities of what an optimized version of psycho-sensory therapy might look like, Dr Ruden developed a brand new set of protocols that featured simple, soothing movements to produce delta waves in the brain that neutralized deeply upsetting or uncomfortable emotions.

By combining these physical movements with eye movements (lateral rather than upwards) and guided visualization, he was able to measurably change the chemical landscape of the brain, stripping the physical markers of the past experience away from the synapses where they had become stored.

In layman's terms, it allows us to separate out the memories from the feelings without any need to relive the unpleasant or traumatic past events that caused them.

How could something so simple be so powerful?

This process, known as Havening, is simple to learn and can be used on almost any problem, block or trauma. Dr Ruden has personally treated over three thousand patients with it, and it is currently being researched by universities around the world as a treatment for PTSD and related issues.

Here are some of the results of one of our pre-trial single-treatment studies done at King's College in London. The percentages represent answers given before treatment (BT), after treatment (AT), and two months after treatment (2M):

Question	BT	AT	2M
How often do you feel bad about yourself?	39 per cent said 'not at all'	81 per cent said 'not at all'	77 per cent said 'not at all'
How often do you have trouble oncentrating?	39 per cent said 'not at all'	81 per cent said 'not at all'	93 per cent said 'not at all'
How often do you feel nervous, anxious or on edge?	30 per cent said 'more than half the time'	12.5 per cent said 'more than half the time'	6.7 per cent said 'more than half the time'
How often do you have unwanted images or memories that are distressing?	33 per cent said 'often'	6 per cent said 'often'	3.4 per cent said 'often'
To what extent are you having repeated, disturbing memories or thoughts?	30 per cent said 'quite a bit'	0 per cent said 'quite a bit'	0 per cent said 'quite a bit'

What this means is that nearly everyone was able to boost their self-esteem, concentrate better, eliminate worry and let go of disturbing thoughts after only one session, and that nearly all of them were still benefiting from those changes two months later.

While the research is ongoing, this is the most powerful technique by far that I have ever encountered in the treatment of trauma or mental blocks.

PTSD, chronic pain and hope for humanity

I'll be talking more about the science behind Havening in the next chapter, and there are a number of evidence-based research projects taking place at the moment at universities and hospitals around the world to verify its efficacy. But to a non-medical therapist like me, the anecdotal stories are the most powerful. I have personally treated thousands of people using the Havening technique, and some of the changes I've witnessed have moved me to tears.

I was teaching a seminar for medical doctors on Havening and put out a request for someone who had a severe case of PTSD, because Dr Ruden and I wanted to demonstrate just how powerful and quick a process it is. A soldier in his early thirties volunteered to come on to the seminar as a test subject.

He was in the bomb-disposal unit of the British Army, serving in Northern Ireland, when he was sent to deal with a bomb explosion at a hospital. When they entered the hospital, a secondary device went off, killing two men in his immediate vicinity, including the father of a little girl, who lay crying and screaming between him and her dead father. For the next ten years, he woke up every night at 4 a.m., sobbing and shaking as he saw the little girl's face and heard the sounds of her screams in his mind.

He tried every available therapy from counselling to Cognitive-Behavioural Therapy to EMDR, but nothing made any difference. I worked with him in front of the group for

73 minutes, explaining the process to the doctors in the audience as I took him through it. By the time we had completed the process, he appeared to be totally cured. One year later, he is still completely free from PTSD, and he no longer wakes up in the middle of the night distressed. He can still remember that a terrible event occurred, but the sadness, anger and panic attacks that haunted him have gone for ever and he lives a happy and fulfilling life.

At another event, I asked for somebody who had chronic pain. A lady volunteered who had, for a number of years, experienced pain in her legs, yet there was no discernible medical reason why. I began the Havening process with her, stroking the sides of her arms, asking her to visualize different things. While the pain reduced, it wouldn't entirely disappear.

Suddenly, the woman began to cry and she said to me, 'Something really bad happened to me in my childhood.'

I said, 'I don't need to know anything about it in order to help you,' and with her permission began Havening it.

After about 20 minutes more in front of a room of assembled doctors, psychologists and psychiatrists, she said with surprise in her voice, 'I feel fine – the pain has gone! I can remember that something bad happened, but I don't feel the physical or emotional pain any more.'

Havening is going to change the entire face of psychology, and soon you will join the thousands of people who are already benefiting from it. I now frequently work with people who have experienced extreme trauma – war veterans, bereavement and all manner of personal crises – and often after only a single treatment they tell me, 'How is it possible that I felt so bad for so long, and now suddenly I'm free?'

I tell them what I would like to tell you – it's because of the genius algorithm created by Dr Ruden, which is deceptively simple but creates an extraordinary and measurable physiological change in the structure of the brain. As a result, we now have a simpler and more reliable way than ever before to clear the traumas of the past and give people a fresh start for the future.

Time for a change

Over the next two chapters, I'll share more of the science behind Havening and prepare you for your personal session with me on the DVD/download. We will sit down together and I'll take you through the entire process from beginning to end. You can reuse this technique as often as you like on as many different blocks or traumas from the past as you can find. Over time, you'll find that the process begins to generalize and you can clear any number of different things simultaneously in a matter of minutes. This will enable you to come to life with less baggage and more of your natural resources than ever before.

Here's what's important to remember going forward:

- **Havening is a scientifically tested model based on the latest research into brain science and change.**

- **For the purposes of our work together, a 'trauma' is simply any past experience that has been coded in your brain as a potential future threat.**

- **I will personally guide you through every step of the process. All you need to do is follow along with the DVD.**

CHAPTER FIVE

•

Nature vs Nurture

AN IMPORTANT NOTE

In this chapter, I'm going to be sharing a bit of what I've learned about the science behind human potential and how change happens. You don't need to understand this to benefit from it, so if you'd like to skip ahead to the next chapter, you can. However, **IT IS ESSENTIAL YOU READ CHAPTER SIX AND DO THE HAVENING TECHNIQUE ON THE DVD/DOWNLOAD**. This is in many ways the most important exercise in the whole book, and what you read in that chapter will help you to benefit from it even more than if you simply dive straight into the technique.

Is destiny in our genes?

For many years, I have begun my talks and seminars about the power of the mind by sharing the analogy of the brain as the fastest-processing and largest-capacity supercomputer in the world. But over the past few years I've had the privilege of learning from some of the brightest minds in the fields of epigenetics and neuroscience about how the mind and body work together to create our health and well-being. What I've come to see is that the human system is more impressive than I'd ever imagined.

Dr Bruce Lipton is a cellular biologist whose ground-breaking book *The Biology of Belief* introduced the extraordinary science of epigenetics to the mainstream world. Epigenetics is the study of how our genes are impacted on by our environment. In Dr Lipton's case, his breakthrough came when he was doing stem cell research at Stanford University's School of Medicine.

He placed one stem cell into a culture dish and it divided every ten hours. After only two weeks, there were thousands of genetically identical cells in the dish, all exact duplicates of the original. He then divided the cells into three separate culture dishes and manipulated the environment that contained the cells in each dish. In one dish, the cells became bone, in another, fat, and in the third, muscle. In other words, the genes (which, remember, were all identical) didn't determine what they turned into – their environment did.

Here's why this matters to us, in Dr Lipton's own words:

With fifty trillion cells in your body, the human body is the equivalent of a skin-covered petri dish. Moving your body from one environment to another alters the composition of the 'culture medium,' the blood. The chemistry of the body's culture medium determines the nature of the cell's environment within you. The blood's chemistry is largely impacted by the chemicals emitted from your brain. Brain chemistry adjusts the composition of the blood based upon your perceptions of life.

So this means that your perception of any given thing, at any given moment, can influence the brain chemistry, which, in turn, affects the environment where your cells reside and controls their fate. In other words, your thoughts and perceptions have a direct and overwhelmingly significant effect on cells.

What this means is that our mind impacts our bodies at a cellular, even genetic level. The perception in your mind is directly reflected in the chemistry of your body, and you can literally change the fate of your cells by altering your thoughts. Our destiny is not fixed, even at a biological level. Dr Lipton says:

You can rewire yourself. (First) you must recognize that you are a participant in the unfolding of your life. Then you can go into your subconscious program and find out where the problems are.

His research suggests that the subconscious mind learns from patterns and repetition of patterns. By accessing that deeper mind, we can rewrite those habits. The million-pound question is, how?

In order to better answer that question, let's take a look at how those patterns get locked into the subconscious in the first place.

A bit of brain science

One of the oldest parts of the brain is collectively known as the limbic system. The limbic system is often called 'the emotional system', as it controls our moods, emotions and motivation for success. At the heart of this system are two tiny little bundles of cells that live on each side of the brain behind the ear, and are collectively known as the amygdala.

The amygdala is the central processing unit of the brain for emotional memory storage and retrieval. The brain relies on those memories to tell us what is dangerous and what to avoid – when to flee and when to fight. The amygdala acts as a sort of on/off switch for our sympathetic nervous system – the part of the brain that controls the fight or flight response. When the amygdala perceives a threat, a host of brain chemicals – adrenaline, noradrenaline, dopamine, cortisol and more – get released into the body.

In case of an actual emergency, these chemicals make our bodies stronger and our minds sharper. Adrenaline energizes the body, while noradrenaline does the same for the mind, helping us focus and even taking away the sensation of pain in extreme circumstances. Adrenaline also gives strength to the muscles and increases our take-up of blood sugar so that we have more 'fast-burn' energy.

But the amygdala is also the place where traumas from the past get encoded into the brain. And since, once a trauma is encoded in the brain, the amygdala has no way to tell the difference between a real threat in the moment and an imagined threat based on a past trauma, we often wind up all revved up with no place to go. This 'over-firing' of the sympathetic nervous system can lead to chronic stress, illness, depression and a limited sense of possibility for your life.

Making a crisis out of a drama

In Dr Ruden's research into the impact of stored trauma on the human nervous system, he has identified four conditions that need to be present for an emotional or stressful event to turn into a full-blown trauma:

1. **The event must be seen as important or meaningful.**
2. **The event must be perceived emotionally, not just rationally.**
3. **The landscape of the brain must be receptive to fresh programming.**
4. **There must be a feeling of inescapability to the stress or emotion.**

So what gets stored in your brain as a 'trauma' can be something as innocuous as a bad argument with a parent or friend or something as dramatic as being a victim of a crime or witnessing an accident. If these things happen to you at a time when you are otherwise high-functioning, chances are they won't get stored as traumas in the brain. But there are numerous circumstances where the likelihood of an amygdalic imprint are heightened:

Puberty
Lack of confidence
Lack of education
Low self-esteem
High or continual stress
Poor living conditions
Ill-health
Over-sensitivity
High empathy
In the wake of a major life event

While none of these conditions in and of themselves cause an experience to be stored as a trauma, they are contributory factors. And once the memory has been stored as a traumatic one, it will remain in that category in spite of pretty much any attempt to shift it through controlling our thoughts or emotions. It has become a physical coding in the brain itself, and will have a life of its own up until something outside the brain acts on it.

This is why no matter how hard we try to rationalize away our fears, they just won't shift – the problem exists at a deeper level than simple logical argument, positive thinking or personal will can get to.

Dr Ruden has made an astounding scientific breakthrough, and in the next chapter I will share with you how Havening works to clear stored trauma from the amygdala and frees us up to have a fresh start in life. Then, in the final chapter of this section, I will outline the actual Havening process that you and I will go through together on the accompanying DVD/download.

It is very important that you both read through the next chapter AND take the time to go through the process with me on the video, which contains everything I would do with you if we were working together in person. While simply reading about it may be enjoyable, it is necessary to physically engage with the process to experience the full effect.

Here's what you'll want to remember from this chapter:

- **The perception in your mind is directly reflected in the chemistry of your body, and you can literally change the fate of your cells by altering your thoughts.**

- **Our destiny is not fixed, even at a biological level.**

- **No matter how hard we try to rationalize away our fears, they often stay with us. This is because they have a physical component that simple logical argument, positive thinking or personal will can't reach.**

- **Havening is a simple and more reliable way than ever before to clear the traumas of the past and give people (including you!) a fresh start for the future.**

CHAPTER SIX

•

Creating a
Safe Haven

A higher goal

For many years, the goal of my work was to help people get more control – over their levels of happiness, their health, their finances and, perhaps most often, their weight. By gaining a deeper understanding of the structure of someone's subjective experience, I could share with them better and better ways to take charge of that experience, and leave them with a choice in relation to whatever it was they wanted to do, be or have.

Yet as I've learned more about what it is that unites us as human beings, I've come to realize that what people really want is freedom – 'freedom from' and 'freedom to'. They want freedom from the overwhelm and stress that seem to come standard with any level of achievement in life. Freedom from the habits of their own brain chemistry that make them blush when they want to appear cool and panic when they would prefer to stay calm.

And they also want the freedom to go for what they want without worrying about being miserable if they don't get it first time around. The freedom to approach a potential client for a sale or a potential lover for a date without being held back by fear or anxiety. The freedom to live happily in the world without worrying about the psychological bogeymen of their thinking dragging them back down into sadness, despair or depression.

Since we are about to do our very first Havening session together, take a few moments now to think about what you would most like freedom from or freedom to. This could be an emotion you currently feel stuck with, one that arises each time you're faced with your most distressing personal issues or a particular challenge. It could also be a block – something that holds you back even if you don't know what it is or where it comes from.

Write down at least three stuck emotions, past traumas or blocks that hold you back in your life today. These will be the content for our first session together on the DVD/download:

1. _____

2. _____

3. _____

Remember, even after Havening you will still retain a memory of the event and any insight you gained from the incidents in your past, they simply will no longer be able to create stress in your body or depress the neurochemical landscape of your brain.

A step-by-step guide

I am now going to walk you through the steps of the Havening process. However, *please do not attempt to use these steps yourself unless you have already done the guided Havening process with me at least three full times.* This section is designed to be a sort of 'preview of coming attractions' rather than a 'how-to' manual. I will tell you what we will be doing and a little bit about why we will be doing it. When you sit down to work with the recorded session, I will take you through the process in real time!

Step 1: What would you like more freedom around?

Choose one of the stuck emotions, past traumas or limiting blocks you highlighted in the last section and take a moment to feel what it feels like in your body. Notice how much discomfort, sadness, anger or fear you feel and rate it on a scale of 1 to 10. As you're doing the process, you will notice the rate and speed at which it's reducing.

This step gives us a specific focus for our session and sets a number as a starting point for comparison. We will come back to this number several times during the process to measure progress.

Step 2: Clear your mind

I will then ask you to clear your mind, or just think about something nice and pleasant.

Unlike traditional forms of therapy, with Havening we don't want you to feel bad a moment longer than you have to. After all, the goal of Havening is freedom from limiting emotions, so it makes little sense to indulge in them a moment longer than is needed.

Step 3: A gentle touch and visualization

When I tell you, cross your arms, place your hands on the tops of your shoulders and close your eyes. Begin stroking the sides of your arms, from the shoulders down to the elbows. As you do, imagine walking along a beach or down a flight of stairs and count out loud from 1 to 20 with each step you take.

What Dr Ruden discovered is that patterns of repeated touch to parts of the body combined with specific (lateral) eye movements and visualizations have a rapid, reliable and predictable effect on our feelings. The patterns of touch used in Havening are what enable a mother to comfort her baby and they are hard-wired into every infant. Havening combines these deep-rooted patterns of reassurance and comfort with sequences to break down the associations that triggered unhappy feelings. As a result, in just a few minutes we can now reduce the intensity of an emotion or feeling of unhappiness and establish calm, robust relaxation.

Step 4: Advanced lateral eye movement desensitization

Next I will ask you to open your eyes and move them laterally to the right and then to the left several times as you continue to stroke the sides of your arms from shoulder to elbow.

When measured in brain scans, horizontal eye movements were found to produce delta waves in the brain. Delta is the deepest level of relaxation, normally only found in deep sleep, and is ideal for reprogramming the mind and body.

Step 5: More gentle touch and visualization

Finally, I will ask you to close your eyes and once again imagine you are walking along a beach, going down a flight of stairs or swimming in a pool, counting aloud as you continue to gently stroke the sides of your arms.

This technique is not merely a distraction. Studies have shown that when we use the Havening technique we reduce stress chemicals in our body and produce states of relaxation and calm. We also change the way our brain processes thoughts and feelings.

Step 6: Check your progress and repeat as needed

When you have completed step 5, I will tell you to open your eyes and check, on your scale from 1 to 10, the number of the feeling now. If it is above a 1 or a 2, you will simply go back and repeat the steps.

We will continue this process of arm stroking and visualization with eye-movement desensitization until you feel better. Once the scale is right down at the bottom, congratulations – you have changed your state and that, in turn, will change your decisions, your behaviour and your destiny!

Let's get to it . . .

There is no point in going ahead with the book until you have done this exercise at least once. Even if you don't feel you have anything from the past that holds you back, choose any area of your life where you'd like to experience more freedom and take 15 minutes now to change your life for ever.

> *I promise you that the little bit of time and effort it takes to participate in this process will be rewarded beyond your wildest dreams!*

After you've completed the exercise at least once, you can review these key points and move on to the second thing:

- **Our goal in clearing up the limiting associations of your past is freedom – the freedom from chronic or habitual unpleasant emotions and the freedom to live your life on your terms in pursuit of what matters most.**

- **Even after Havening you will still retain some of the memory and knowledge you gained from the incidents in your past – they will simply no longer be able to create stress in your body or depress the neurochemical landscape of your brain.**

- **If you want to change your destiny, you need to take the time to actually do the exercises provided on the accompanying DVD/CD/downloads!**

THE SECOND THING

•

SUPERCHARGING
THE PRESENT

*'The point of power is always in
the present moment.'*
LOUISE HAY

CHAPTER SEVEN

•

Your Best Self

The precious present

Years ago, a friend showed me a picture of two circles side by side on a piece of paper. The first one had a narrow horizontal band across the middle; the second featured parallel lines near the top and bottom of the circle:

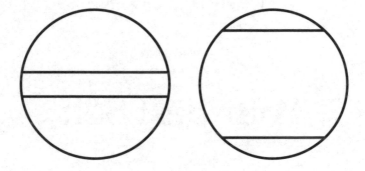

He told me that they represented the two ways people tend to live their lives. He then wrote the words 'Past', 'Present', and 'Future' into the first circle:

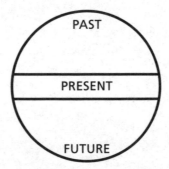

'Most people spend their lives obsessing about the past or worrying about the future. The present is like a thin band of time to them, almost incidental to the quality of their lives.'

He then filled in the second circle in the same way:

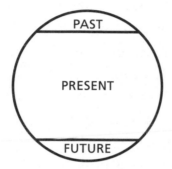

'It is very rare that you find someone who has learned to live their life fully in the here and now. But as you can know, what you focus on grows – and the more of your attention you put on your life in the present, the richer your present becomes.'

Living more in the moment doesn't take away your memories of the past or your ability to create a positive future – it just means that you will get more out of yourself and your life on a daily basis.

For the next few chapters, I'll be sharing some of the most powerful strategies for getting the most out of each and every day of your life. You'll learn to expand and optimize your sense of self, get luckier, get more in touch with your deepest values and live your perfect day again and again in your mind until it begins to be your reality.

The unbreakable human spirit

I love remarkable stories, and the story of Louis Zamperini is one of the most remarkable I have ever heard. As a working-class kid born and raised in southern California, Louis grew up in and out of trouble with the law. But by the time he was 19, he'd taken up sport, and he competed in the 1936 Olympic Games in Berlin. He came in tenth place, but was fast enough to get a congratulatory handshake from Hitler and brave enough to climb a guarded flagpole and steal Hitler's personal flag.

When the second world war came along, Louis became a soldier and worked as a bombardier on a B-24 flying out of Hawaii. Then his life changed for ever. His plane crashed in the middle of the Pacific, and alongside two of his crewmates he ate birds and fought off sharks to survive for more than six weeks.

Louis and his one surviving companion drifted west in their life raft over 2,000 miles before washing ashore in the Marshall Islands and being taken prisoner by the Japanese. For two years, he was singled out for both physical and psychological torture by a guard who mocked his athletic past by forcing him to do push-ups over pits of human excrement.

But in spite of all of that, he never once broke, refusing to the very end to broadcast anti-American propaganda on behalf of his captors. And unlike many soldiers who never fully recovered from the ordeals of war, Louis Zamperini lived a productive life in his native southern California until the end of his days at the age of 97. He has been called 'a virtuoso of joy'. His story has been the subject of two books and the recent movie *Unbroken* – and it is a testament to the incredible human potential that lives inside every one of us.

Tapping into a deeper potential

What is it that allowed someone like Louis Zamperini to survive some of the most devastating conditions known to man while others are defeated before the first shot is even fired?

It is an attitude of mind. 'Attitude' literally means 'angle of approach', and when it comes to the human potential, it is consistently one of the differences that makes the difference between a top performer in any field and an also-ran. Fortunately, it is something that can be learned, practised and ultimately developed within ourselves.

In my hypnosis seminars, I often do an exercise called Deep Trance Identification. In order to deep-trance-identify with someone they would like to learn from, it is simply necessary for the participant to be familiar with that person's work. Ideally they will have read numerous books about them, watched them on video and/or listened to recordings of them.

I then relax them into trance and instruct their unconscious minds to 'become' the person, a bit like the way a method actor fully immerses themselves into a character. They begin to move their body the way that person moves and speak the way they speak and suddenly they begin to exhibit the same amazing quality of thought and energy their role model has.

In doing what at first might seem to some like a simple impersonation, they become more confident, optimistic, creative or intelligent. By taking on the physiology and speech of the person, they gain access to the same quality of thoughts.

What I've learned over the years is that you don't need to go into a deep trance in order to get the benefits of this exercise. You can use a simpler and more accessible version of this psychological technique to gain a new perspective or insight into any area you would like to explore. You simply imagine 'stepping in' to somebody who is skilled at the area you are exploring and then looking at your present situation 'through their eyes'. Here is all you need to do:

ROLE MODEL STEP IN

1. Close your eyes and imagine that the person whose attitude and perspective you would most like to benefit from is standing in front of you.

2. For example, you might want to learn about:
   - resilience from Louis Zamperini
   - love from Shakespeare
   - creativity from Leonardo da Vinci
   - business from Richard Branson
   - spirituality from the Dalai Lama

3. In your imagination, float into their body and see and hear things the way they would see and hear them.

4. Focus on whatever quality you are cultivating in yourself and notice what insights you get.

5. From the perspective of your role model, ask yourself each of the following questions:
   - What should I do more of?
   - What should I do less of?
   - What should I start doing?
   - What should I stop doing?

6. Take action on your best insights as soon as you possibly can!

While you can try this on your own, when I take you through it on the video we will add in another step as I guide you into your ultimate self. Each time you repeat this technique, you will grow in confidence, optimism and resilience as you tap into more of your potential!

Here are a few things worth bearing in mind from this chapter:

- **'Attitude' literally means 'angle of approach', and it is something that can be learned, practised and ultimately developed within ourselves.**

- **We can learn from the attitudes and perceptions of our heroes and role models, finding in ourselves what is in them.**

- **We are capable of so much more than we think.**

CHAPTER EIGHT

•

How to Get Lucky

The luck filter

My friend Professor Richard Wiseman has been researching luck for more than a decade and he has collected significant evidence that shows that lucky people meet their perfect partners, achieve their lifelong ambitions, find fulfilling careers and live happy and meaningful lives. Their success is not due to them working especially hard, being amazingly talented or exceptionally intelligent. Instead, they simply appear to have an uncanny ability to be in the right place at the right time.

The results of his research reveal that people are not born lucky. Instead, lucky people are, often without even realizing it, guided by their belief in themselves as lucky to think and behave in ways that create good fortune in their lives.

Often, they have been told that they are lucky from an early age, or they experienced several positive events over a short period of time that left them with the feeling of being lucky or blessed. These experiences shape their internal filters for reality, and the belief in their own luck sets their mind up to seek opportunities and support them in rising to challenges.

These positive internal filters lead to a relaxed approach to life and an openness to new experiences. 'Lucky' people trust their intuition and gut feelings, and are even more likely to meditate or apply other techniques to boost their already good fortune.

Since they 'know' in their minds that they are fundamentally lucky, they look forward to the future because they assume it will be filled with good fortune. These assumptions become expectations, which in turn become self-fulfilling prophecies. Since people who believe themselves to be lucky are optimistic about how things will turn out, they tend to be positive in their interactions with others and foster the very conditions that make a positive outcome more likely.

In the same way, because lucky people always expect things to turn out in their favour in the end, when ill-fortune comes their way, they are automatically and naturally able to re-frame it and ride things out until the tide turns back in their favour. This makes them appear to be remarkably resilient, even in the face of the kinds of negative life events that all human beings run into from time to time.

In one particularly interesting experiment, Professor Wiseman asked subjects to flip through a newspaper and count the number of photographs inside it. Unbeknown to the subjects, after about three pages there was a massive half-page advert that said, 'Stop counting – there are 43 photographs in this newspaper.' In case they missed it, a few pages later there was another massive advert that said, 'Stop counting. Tell the experimenter you've seen this and win 150 pounds!'

For the most part, people who had identified themselves as unlucky missed both of these adverts. The lucky people would flip through, laugh and say, 'There are 43 photos. That's what it says. Do you want me to bother counting?'

When told to carry on, they'd flip some more and say, 'Do I get my 150 pounds?'

In other words, the people who *believed* they were lucky experienced greater success because the lucky filter in their minds alerted them to notice and seize the opportunity in front of them.

Most interestingly of all, whether or not a person considers themselves to be lucky appears to be the critical factor in the extent to which they benefit from these perceptual filters. At the end of the chapter, I will help you to install a 'luck filter' in your unconscious mind so that you will automatically see and seize wonderful, life-enhancing, positive opportunities, more and more of the time!

Beyond physics

Although self-perception is a huge part of luck, there is another element to it. It takes a little more understanding to make sense of this with conventional science.

I have a friend who owns a casino, and he told me about people who are employed as 'coolers'. These are self-declared unlucky people who are so convinced of their bad luck that it becomes a self-fulfilling prophecy. Bizarrely, they can statistically lower the chances of winning of the people playing near them – literally 'cooling them off' in the midst of a hot streak at the tables.

How is this possible?

Many people believe that the universe unfolds simultaneously on two levels – the physical, and the energetic, or metaphysical. ('Metaphysical' simply means 'beyond the physical'.) We know that the universe is made up of atoms and molecules vibrating at different frequencies. Inside the atoms are quarks; inside the quarks are, as far as we can tell, absolutely nothing. So everything is ultimately made of this energy, vibrating at different rates and speeds.

And, in the same way, a human being is constantly vibrating on an emotional frequency, like a radio station. So, on an energetic level, people who believe they're lucky are literally sending out a different signal into the universe.

I first started thinking about how people could incorporate luck as a factor in their personal success when I was watching an interview with Keith Richards from back in the 1970s. The interviewer said to him that there was a list of the people in rock and roll most likely to die young, and that he was on the very top of the list. When the interviewer pushed the question and said, 'Aren't you concerned?', all Richards had to say was, 'Well, my luck hasn't run out yet.'

And I thought to myself: 'Well, if luck is an energy, why can't we harness it?'

Lucky for life!

The technique I am going to take you through in a few moments is one of my all-time favorites. I have used it to change my own luck for the better, and I have tested it on hundreds of people with astounding results. An actor I worked with did the exercise every day for a week and landed a hit TV show before a month had passed. A man who had been continually unlucky in love surprised himself and everyone who knew him by meeting the girl of his dreams and getting married. An executive finally got a well-deserved promotion after years of being passed over for her less talented colleagues, and, over the course of a year, a bankrupted entrepreneur began spotting new opportunities and built a new business that is now worth over seven figures.

It's a simple visualization technique that resets your perceptual filters by vividly recalling times when you felt everything was going your way, or when you felt particularly lucky. I will then guide you to reset your filters and re-code how you think and feel about your relationship with luck and life.

Many people start to notice amazing changes in how they feel almost immediately, and their ability to spot opportunities greatly increases. Stranger still, more opportunities curiously begin to find them.

Here's how it works:

First, I will ask you to remember a time or series of times where it felt like everything was going your way. You'll amplify the memories so that the feeling of good fortune will be radiating throughout your body and you feel really, really good.

We will continue to intensify the feeling until you are ready to burst with positive sensations, and then we will explode that lucky energy into every area of your life!

When you're ready to experience this for yourself, go to the DVD or video download and click on the track marked *Change Your Luck – Change Your Life!*

Can it be this simple?

People sometimes ask me if I really believe that becoming luckier is enough to change their destiny. While all of the exercises in this book are part of a larger system, becoming luckier has been one of the most powerful change processes I have used in my own life.

Here are a few things to bear in mind as we move ahead:

- **Scientific research shows that people who think of themselves as lucky consistently experience more luck in their lives.**

- **Luck is a state of mind created by a set of perceptual filters and carries with it an energetic vibration.**

- **You can change your level of luck and reap the benefits in every area of your life!**

CHAPTER NINE

•

What Matters to You?

The value of values

For the first part of my adult life, I was a very goal-driven person. Everything that happened in my life was filtered through the lens of my future plans – was this something that was taking me closer to the life of my dreams, or further away?

As I got a bit older and began crossing more and more things off my goal list, I began to see that I was caught in a trap. No matter how good things got, I was always putting off being truly satisfied until the next thing on my list was achieved.

Then one day a new question occurred to me:

For the sake of what?

Why was I working so hard? Why did it matter if the next goal was achieved, or the one after that?

I realized I'd fallen into the trap of working so hard for my future that my present was being left behind. So I took a bit of time out to see what was most important to me.

I made a list of everything that mattered to me – love, happiness, family, achievement, loyalty, health and more. If there was something on the list that was more of a 'thing' than a feeling – such as 'money', or 'success' – I asked myself what it was about that thing that I valued. For example, money gave me a sense of security, and success gave me a feeling of satisfaction in a job well done.

In the end, I had about a dozen things on my list that came up again and again.

Next, I began to list these 'values' from most to least

important. I would compare two things that both mattered to me and imagine I could only have one of them. 'Health' quickly rode its way towards the top of the list, but 'love', 'happiness' and 'fulfilment' beat it out for the top spots.

Finally, when I had a 'top four', I made a simple commitment to myself: every day, I would do whatever I could to tick the box for each one of my top values.

Did I experience love today?
Did I experience laughter?
Did I experience joy?
Did I experience a sense of giving something
of value to the world?

I knew that once I was living a life that was driven by my values, whether or not I could get the world to conform to my expectations, I would be able to feel good about myself, because I was living what was most important to me. I would be a living embodiment of everything that made me feel good.

That's a commitment to myself I've done a pretty good job at keeping – and the quality of my daily life has been the reward.

To experience the power of spending your daily allotment of time in the service of what matters most to you, take a few minutes now to identify your core values. Then, on the DVD/download, I will take you through an exercise called *Living Your Values* where you will spread the positive feelings of the things that matter most to you into every area of your life:

LIVING YOUR VALUES

1. Think about what it is that you value most in life and make a list below. Here are some questions to help you:
    *   What's most important to you?
    *   What kind of a person would you like to be remembered as?
    *   Who do you really respect in life? What is it about them that you respect most?
    *   What do you most prize?
    *   What do you most like about yourself?
    *   What do you consider to be your top five achievements?
    *   Why?

2. Now you should have a list of words that represent what matters most to you. Next, what I'd like you to do is order them in a hierarchy, with the most important ones at the top.
    *   Ask yourself, would I rather have 'x' or 'y'?
    *   If you can't decide, imagine that you were only able to have one of them – which would you choose?

3. Write down your revised list below.

Your perfect day

Many people ask me what's the single most important thing I've learned in over twenty years of working with people on having better, happier, richer and more successful lives. While it's difficult to narrow it down to just one thing, if I had to choose, I would choose this:

You get more of what you focus on!

If you focus on what you don't want, you will begin to notice it everywhere; if you focus on what you do want, that too will begin to become your world.

One of the most useful ways to take advantage of the power of focus is by imagining your perfect day again and again in your mind until elements of it start appearing in your world. This is not a day filled with specific outcomes, but rather a day where you live your values fully and completely.

When I first began doing this exercise, I imagined a day where I spent a lot of time laughing with friends, feeling love, being creative and sharing with the world. I imagined myself healthy and filled with energy, transforming lives and having a wonderful time doing it.

I imagined myself bringing humour and hope into challenging situations, solving problems that at first seemed beyond me and turning things around even when, at first glance, all appeared to be lost.

Finally, I imagined myself drifting off to sleep with the woman I love at my side, feeling happy and fulfilled, with a sense of having had a wonderful day and the certainty that tomorrow will once again bring with it a host of opportunities, challenges to be met and one or two delightful surprises as well.

When you do the *Living Your Values* exercise on the video, you will also get the opportunity to create *Your Perfect Day*. You may be surprised at how quickly elements of the perfect day you imagined begin showing up in your real life!

From past to present to future

At this point in the book, you should already be feeling quite differently to how you were when we began. We have cleared away some of your more traumatic memories from the past, and showed you how to access more of your resources in the present.

Before we begin to create a new, powerful future, take a few moments to reflect on these key points:

- **When we expand the present, we have more power available to us to do whatever it is we want to do.**

- **Anyone you admire or respect is reflecting a quality or characteristic you can develop in yourself.**

- **What matters most must never be at the mercy of what matters least.**

- **If you live your values every single day, you will become a living embodiment of everything that makes you feel wonderful!**

THE THIRD THING

•

CREATING
THE FUTURE

'The best way to predict the future is to create it.'
PETER DRUCKER

CHAPTER TEN

•

A Gentle Walk Into the Future

A life without regrets

There was a report on Radio 4 last year that focused on elderly people who were near the end of their lives, asking them about their biggest regrets. Number one on the list was that they wished they had spent less time worrying. In a similar vein, Australian care worker Bronnie Ware wrote a bestselling book outlining the five things that her patients consistently said they regretted as they came to the end of their life:

- **They wish they'd had the courage to live a life true to themselves, not the life others expected of them.**
- **They wish they hadn't worked so hard.**
- **They wish they'd had the courage to express their feelings.**
- **They wish they had stayed in touch with their friends.**
- **They wish they had let themselves be happier.**

What I've learned in my 25 years of working with hypnosis and positive psychology is that the unconscious mind cannot process a negative directly. So if somebody asks you to try not to think of an elephant, you need to first imagine the elephant in order to know what not to think about.

This is because the mind thinks at least partially in pictures, whether we are aware of those pictures or not. For example, in order to answer the question, 'What colour is your front door?', you first make a picture of it in your mind's eye. The mind is designed to seek out ways to create in the world the pictures we carry most consistently in our heads. This is why when you think about buying something new, you begin to see that thing everywhere you go. Holding the picture sets a filter for it in your mind.

This function of the mind, often referred to as the Reticular Activating System, or RAS, acts like a heat-seeking missile, continually making adjustments in mid-flight once it's locked on to its target. It will filter out anything in the world that doesn't match your internal pictures, causing things that will help you reach your goals to 'jump out' at you when you see them.

Some people even believe that the mind can actually create in the world what we hold as possible in our heads. While it is certainly true that everything created in the world started out as an idea in someone's mind, there is no doubt that we get more of what we focus on in life.

If you stop to think about it, everything created in the world once started out as an idea in someone's mind. So when I work with people on creating powerful positive futures, I am quick to point out the value of focusing on what you want, not what you don't want.

For example, a woman came to me once because she 'kept meeting the wrong men'. She could describe these men in great detail, and she told me that, despite all her efforts to avoid them, she somehow kept winding up in relationships with them. Once I explained that the mind will always seek to create the images we hold in our mind, she began to imagine the kind of man she wanted to be with, instead of the kind of man she wanted to avoid. Within a month, she met the man she wound up marrying and they are happily together to this day.

How does all this apply to living a life with no regrets?

Well, if we were to state each of those regrets in terms of their positive opposites, here's what we might wind up with:

- **I want to live a life that's true to myself, regardless of what others expect of me.**
- **I want to work smart, not hard.**
- **I want the people around me to know how I feel about them, especially the people I love and care for.**
- **I want to build deep and lasting friendships.**
- **I want to be happy.**

Each one of these things is now an achievable outcome – a viable way of living in the world.

1. **To live a life that's true to yourself, make sure you're living your values every single day.** This one move will ensure that you're living life on your terms, building your days around what matters most.

2. **To work smart, not hard, apply the 80 / 20 rule.** Since studies show that 80 per cent of your success will come

from 20 per cent of your efforts, do an audit of how you spend your time at work and eliminate as many of the 'low-impact' activities as you can. This will free you up to put extra energy and effort into the high-impact, high-reward activities, increasing your effectiveness while reducing the overall amount of time it takes to get things done.

3. **One of the most impactful exercises I ever did as part of a personal development programme was to make a list of the five people in my life I most love and care for, and to reach out to each one of them with a phone call, email or handwritten note to express my appreciation for them in my life.** Not only did that make a real difference to the quality of our relationships, it gave me an incredible feeling of love and appreciation that I can call on any time I'm feeling a bit disconnected or out of touch.

4. **When I talk to people who have been happily married for ten years or more, they nearly all describe their partner as their best friend in the world.** Friendship is one of the greatest gifts we can experience in our lives, and a good and loyal friend is worth their weight in gold. According to Dr George Pransky, the author of *The Relationship Handbook*, the secret to a great friendship is to put the majority of your attention on

enjoying each other's company. Any time you find yourself getting bogged down in the details of 'who did what to who', reignite your friendship by shifting your focus on to the simple pleasures of hanging out together and having a great time.

5. **Happiness is a state of mind that is available to all of us at any time.** If there is a secret to happiness, I believe it is the same secret I have repeated throughout this book – we get more of what we focus on. So if you want to feel happier more of the time, spend more of your time focusing on those thoughts and things that make you happy!

A life well lived

This next exercise is one of my favourites, and it's extraordinary how much of an impact it can have on your life. I've seen people radically change their behaviour as a result of what they've seen, including turning their backs on bad relationships and recommitting themselves to their health, their friends and their family. I will guide you through it step by step on the accompanying video, and you can return to it at any time.

What I will be asking you to do is to step out into the future and imagine that you are coming towards the latter part of your life and you are truly, deeply happy and content. I will then ask you a series of questions about why you feel so good about the life you have lived. While some of the things you realize may be obvious to you, some of your answers are likely to surprise you.

One of my friends did this exercise when he was in his early twenties and, to his surprise, realized that what he would be most grateful for when he was approaching the end of his life was that he had been there for his children when they were growing up. This didn't fit with his image of himself as a driven, career-oriented person, not to mention the fact that he didn't have any children and was only recently married.

Twenty-five years later, he is now both a successful businessman at the top of his field and one of the happiest family men I know. He credits much of his success in both these areas of his life to the insight he got during this one exercise.

'It really got me to re-evaluate my priorities,' he told me. 'The extra time I spent with my kids did mean that it took me longer to reach a high level in my business than I had originally hoped for. But the relationship I have with my teenage and young adult children is worth every minute, and having such a stable home life has made creating success in my business much easier than I had imagined.'

We are going to do this exercise together now. Please go to the DVD/download and click on the track marked *Life Perspective*. The exercise will take between 5 and 15 minutes to complete, but the difference it makes could last a lifetime!

What would be even better than that?

In the next chapter, I'm going to introduce a bit of a wild card
– something that I have found takes people's lives to a place
they may never have imagined. Before we move forward,
here are a few key points to remember:

- **A bit of thought about your future now can save you a lifetime of regret later.**

- **To work smart, not hard, apply the 80 / 20 rule.**

- **The secret to a great friendship is to put the majority of your attention on enjoying each other's company.**

CHAPTER ELEVEN

•

Your Ultimate Destiny

The enlightened Scotsman

A few years ago, I was told a very strange story that turned out to be completely true. In 1973, a Scottish welder named Sydney Banks with a low-grade education was living and working near Salt Spring Island in British Columbia. He was struggling in his marriage and insecure in his life. In the midst of a conversation with a psychotherapist as part of a weekend encounter group, the psychotherapist said to him, 'You're not insecure, Syd – you just think you are.'

Over the next few days, this simple comment led Syd to a transcendent moment – a glimpse of life beyond the veil of our day-to-day thinking. After having his enlightenment experience, he turned to his wife and told her, 'I've found the true meaning of life. I've found the secret of the mind. We'll be meeting with people from all over the world. I'll be lecturing at universities, and what I've seen will change the face of psychology and psychiatry.'

His wife was initially frightened by this dramatic change in his outlook, but something about Syd's calm certainty and peaceful manner comforted her. As he had predicted, and almost miraculously soon, people from around the world began to arrive at Salt Spring Island to meet the man they had heard could guide them to their own wisdom and a healthier psychological state.

Gurus from India, leaders of self-awareness groups, business executives and doctors, as well as the psychologists and psychiatrists he had predicted, began to seek Syd out to learn what he had to share. Within a short time he was giving lectures to hundreds of people, many of them healthcare professionals who wanted to join him on his quest to share the simple understanding that creates dramatic change, greater peace of mind and surprising insights into their personal and professional lives.

The idea that there was a whole field of psychology that came from the insights of a relatively uneducated Scottish welder fascinated me, and when a friend came back from a four-day intensive raving about the experience and practically glowing with mental health, I had to experience it for myself.

I booked myself in to meet and work with one of Syd's early students, Dr Keith Blevens, who had been working in the trauma ward of a hospital when he first heard about the impact this new understanding of psychology was having. Within a relatively short time, he decided to leave behind his traditional psychotherapeutic training and work with people exclusively using Syd's approach. When I asked him why on earth he would make such a dramatic change, he simply said, 'Results!'

Their work is not technique-based, and so is difficult to capture between the pages of a book, but in essence Syd taught that all our feeling and mental states are created through thought, and that beyond each person's personal thought system there is a reservoir of wisdom, insight and deeper intelligence waiting to be tapped.

My own experience was of an unburdening in my mind and body and what felt like a 'river of insights' into my life that continued for days after my visit. Towards the end of this chapter, I will share with you a technique based on the work of a modern-day Zen master that will give you a glimpse of this reservoir of wisdom and possibility that lives out beyond your personal thinking. Each time you do this technique, it will help you to tap into a deep level of creativity, insight and peace of mind. In the meantime, I'll finish this section with an observation and one of my favourite quotes from Syd.

What's fascinating to me is that Syd Banks wasn't looking for a more spiritual understanding of life; in fact, he had no idea there was anything to look for. The deeper truth of life found him. Here's how he put it:

'Happiness is only ever one thought away – but you must find for yourself that one thought!'

The story of your life

One of the main things I took away from my time learning about Syd's work is that a lot of what I thought was true about my life was just a story I was telling myself. Without even noticing, I had been telling my story so compellingly that I had literally become hypnotized by it. It had become so real I was unable even to see it as a story.

For example, if you were repeatedly told as you were growing up that life is a struggle, chances are that you still experience it that way today. If you were told it was a game, you learned how to play; if you were told it was a journey, you probably have a real sense of how far you've come and how far there still is to go.

Because we all tend to look at the world through the filter of our stories, all we see around us are those 'facts' that validate our story. So, if you've ever wondered why 'things like this' always happen to you, one of the best places to look is at how whatever's happening fits into the story of your life.

What are the things you tell yourself that limit the future you are creating for yourself?

- **The world is a difficult place.**
- **People like me can't get a job/partner/opportunity like that.**
- **There's always too much to do and not enough time.**
- **I already can't cope with all the demands of my life.**

While there may occasionally be some truth to our stories, the more we tell them to ourselves and others, the more real they begin to seem. But no matter how much we believe our stories, they are all still just stories. And the most wonderful thing about a story is that it can be changed, often more easily than you think.

As long as you believe your story is real, you will look outside yourself to make changes. Once you can see that your story, no matter how compelling it may seem, is just the sum total of what you've been telling yourself, you open up the possibility of making changes on the inside that will literally change your world.

If your story says that you are defined by what you have done in the past, you will almost certainly repeat that past on into the future. If you tell yourself a new story about how it's possible to begin doing things differently in any moment, you can change your future, starting right now.

The point is this:

What you think is holding you back from your ultimate destiny is just a story you tell yourself, and you can change that story at any time.

So who are we, really?

Ten years ago, I wrote *Change Your Life in 7 Days* as a sort of summary of the best of what I'd learned about the human potential up to that point in my career. The first chapter was called 'Who are You Really?', and it addressed the gap that often exists between our self-image and our authentic self – who we are when we're at peace with ourselves and are able to 'dance like nobody is watching'.

Since that time, I've come to see that there's an even deeper level to who we are, which in psychology is called the 'transpersonal' level. This is the level beyond our personal thoughts, goals or ego desires, which Syd Banks called 'Universal Mind' and in some Eastern philosophy is called 'Big Mind'.

I truly believe that tapping into this deeper level of mind on a regular basis is not only the most powerful resource we have available to us, it is the key to uncovering our ultimate destiny.

I have been greatly inspired over the past few years by my friendship with Zen master Genpo Roshi. He was staying at my house once and I was expecting him to have a strict schedule of meditations and practices to follow. When I noticed that he didn't seem to be up to much other than enjoying his morning cup of coffee and the view from the balcony looking out over the Hollywood hills, I asked him why he wasn't following a routine.

'The thing is, Paul,' he replied, 'I don't wish to attain anything.'

In order to help people go deep into the transpersonal self, Genpo developed something called the 'Big Mind Process', which I firmly believe is the world's best meditation method. Indeed, initial studies at the University of Utah show that through the Big Mind process, you can achieve a depth of inner peace in minutes that would often have taken a seasoned meditator decades of practice to reach.

On the CD/download, I will guide you through a similar process to give you a taste of that deepest part of who and what we really are. This is not the Big Mind Process, but it is my version and interpretation of his work and is shared with permission. (You can find out more about Genpo's original work at www.BigMind.org.)

As with all the other exercises in this book, in order to get the full value of the experience, it is essential that you do the process in its entirety. It will take you less than 10 minutes to complete, and you can repeat it as often as you like.

The Big Mind Process works on the assumption that there are different parts, or aspects, of the self. For example, there is a part of you that protects you and is continually on the lookout for threats. Another aspect of personality is desire, the part of you that wants things and is willing to do what it takes to get them. Most people also have an 'evaluator' – a part of themselves that is continually judging and evaluating to make sure that things are as they should be.

Each one of these parts is necessary to operate effectively in the world, but collectively they make up the personal self, or ego. The ego is the presentation of who you think you are to the world – that part of you that gets you what you want but needs to be constantly fed or else you start to feel insecure and bad about yourself.

Having an ego is essential to functioning in the world, but it can do its job too well and get in the way of the transpersonal self – that part of us that is connected to a larger whole. In Zen this larger whole is called 'infinite consciousness', or 'the bliss of all bliss'. That's why the goal of Zen practice is to drop the personal self, or ego, long enough to enter the state of no self and experience our true and deeper nature.

While most of us have far too much going on in our personal lives to hang around all day trying to experience 'the bliss of all bliss', it's good for the body, mind and spirit to enter the state of no self at least once a day and reconnect to the infinite. It will make you feel more complete in yourself and more connected with others.

The fact that Genpo has created a way to access that infinite self in only minutes has led to him being seen by some as the most important Buddhist on the planet next to the Dalai Lama.

Others are not so sure. While I am obviously both a friend and a fan, I can see why some more traditional Zen practitioners might consider him controversial. After all, if you've spent 20 years sitting in the lotus position trying to attain enlightenment and someone comes along and teaches complete newcomers how to have a spiritual experience in just a few minutes, it's understandable that you might get upset!

Change your world in 7 minutes

What I have done is used my understanding of NLP and hypnosis to 'compress' the Big Mind Process into a 7-minute trance which allows you to tap into this deepest part of yourself in the midst of even the busiest of lives. Most people experience greater peace the very first time they do it; one person even described it as being 'like touching hands with God'.

As I guide you through the technique on the CD/download, I will be asking you to experience the different aspects of your personality like characters in a play. It's OK if it feels like you're just pretending as you go through this – nearly everyone does at least some of the time, but the results you get as you go deeper into the experience are unmistakably real as your consciousness expands and you feel an extraordinary sense of freedom.

DO THIS EXERCISE NOW!

Here are the most important things to take away from this chapter:

- **It is possible for any one of us to have a destiny-changing insight at any moment, regardless of our background or education.**

- **Happiness is only ever one thought away.**

- **We have both a personal self, or ego, and a transpersonal self, or spirit. Having them in balance is essential to our healthy functioning in the world.**

- **By listening to the *Change Your World in 7 Minutes* technique on the CD/download, you will get many of the benefits of a lifetime of meditation in just minutes a day!**

CHAPTER TWELVE

•

The Future

Starts Now!

Today is the first day of the rest of your life

Just by reading this book and doing the five simple techniques, your life has begun to change for the better. Of course, if you haven't yet done the exercises, it is important to go back and do them now. After all, even the best movie in the world won't do much for you if you don't sit down in front of the screen and watch it.

So, in our final chapter together, I'm going to review the three things we've done and why they are going to have the positive impact on your past, present and future that they will. I'm also going to introduce two additional tools – a *28-Day Journal* and a *Change Your Destiny* hypnotic trance recording – that will help you lock in the changes and take them deeper.

Each of the things we've done – clearing the past, supercharging the present and creating the future – is an essential part of changing your destiny for good.

By **Clearing the past** *through Havening your stuck emotions, memories of trauma and any blocks you might have been experiencing, you free yourself up to experience your life with new eyes. It's like getting a 'mulligan' for life – a fresh start, regardless of what you've been through up to this point in your life.*

Supercharging the present *ensures that each day is its own reward. By stepping into your best self on a regular basis, you begin to get more out of your potential without any additional effort on your part. Shifting your perceptual filters around luck not only feels good, it will cause you to notice every positive thing that happens to you and even see the challenges and dramas of day-to-day living in a more positive light. You'll be surprised at how many things start to come your way each and every day. And by redesigning your life around your values, you'll ensure that no matter where you are in your journey to the future, living well today is its own reward.*

Which brings us to the third thing – **Creating the future**. *On the Change Your Destiny trance on your CD/download, I work with your unconscious mind to place positive images of everything you desire into your future timeline. But in the book I wanted to go about things a bit differently. By stepping out into a happy future, you've discovered not just what you want, but what you need to have the life of your dreams – and now you know, that life will begin to emerge, day by day and moment by moment. And by learning to tap into the deepest part of yourself on a daily basis, you can rest assured that the you who arrives is an even happier and more deeply fulfilled person than the one who set off on the journey.*

For many people, doing an exercise just once acts like a kind of 'magic wand' and is enough to change things for ever. Yet studies have shown that, for about 30 per cent of the population, it is necessary to reinforce the changes through repeated practice. That's why I deliberately made this book short so that you could read it quickly. Most importantly, the key techniques I do with my own clients in private sessions are now available to you at your fingertips – you can use and reuse the videos and audios whenever and wherever you choose!

The power of focus

I have already mentioned several times throughout this book that if I could only share one idea with people, it would be that what we focus on, we get more of. An example of this is this rule, which is taught in MBA programmes and written about in business books the world over:

What gets measured, gets done.

There are two ways we are going to measure your progress going forward as your new destiny begins to unfold. In a few moments I'm going to be asking you to repeat the 'Snapshot in Time' exercise we did at the beginning of the book. This will give you a glimpse of how things are already starting to look different to you.

Then, in the back of the book, you will find a 28-day journal. Each day, I'll be asking you to write down at least 3 new things that you've noticed about yourself or your life. This may be a new behaviour that you noticed came naturally to you, or a different way of being in an old, familiar situation.

Perhaps you found yourself being more confident at a party or social gathering, or standing up for yourself at work or while running errands. Maybe you noticed yourself living one of your values in the midst of a busy day, found a 'lucky' penny in the street, or just realized that things have been going your way without your having to try harder or deliberately do things differently. What's important is that it's something new, different, fun or surprising.

By writing down what happens, you are telling your mind to notice change – and by focusing on positive change, the positive changes will grow. As my friend Michael Neill often asks his clients, 'Wouldn't it be a shame to have a wonderful life and not notice?'

To maximize the impact of what we've done together, I've also made suggestions each day in the journal of which of the exercises from the book to repeat. While the *Change Your World in 7 Minutes* recording and *Change Your Destiny* trance are designed to be used daily, many of the other exercises increase in impact the more you do them. The *Change Your Luck – Change Your Life* exercise in particular seems to cross some kind of a threshold after a week of daily repetition.

You can use the pages in the book to fill in your answers, or you can buy an inexpensive notebook or a fancy journal if you prefer. What's important is that you take the time to write down what you've noticed. It is the act of recording that resets the perceptual filter in the brain and amplifies the positive effects of everything we've done together.

Back to the future

Now it's time to test our work – to see how your perception of your past, present and future have begun to change. While some people are tempted to skip this step in case they haven't really changed and are worried they'll feel bad about themselves, I strongly encourage you to do it anyway.

While sometimes people experience dramatic shifts, a subtle change in the moment can change everything over time. For example, there is usually less than a 1 per cent difference between the times of a gold and silver medallist in an Olympic race, yet that difference makes the difference between being a champion and an also-ran.

An aeroplane that makes even a 5 per cent change in course during a long-haul flight is liable to find itself landing in an entirely different country, and taking 10 per cent of your income and putting it into savings and investments has made thousands of people into millionaires over time.

Remember, change nearly always happens from the inside out. So by checking to see how your perceptions have shifted, you're getting a sneak preview of how your life and destiny will change on the outside over time.

THE CIRCLE OF LIFE, REVISITED

- On a scale from 1 to 10, how would you rate your **health**? How would you have rated it ten years ago? If you continue on the path you're on, how do you suspect you'll rate it ten years from now?

- On a scale from 1 to 10, how would you rate your **relationships**? How would you have rated them ten years ago? If you continue on the path you're on, how do you suspect you'll rate them ten years from now?

- On a scale from 1 to 10, how would you rate your **career**? How would you have rated it ten years ago? If you continue on the path you're on, how do you suspect you'll rate it ten years from now?

- On a scale from 1 to 10, how would you rate your **finances**? How would you have rated them ten years ago? If you continue on the path you're on, how do you suspect you'll rate them ten years from now?

- On a scale from 1 to 10, how would you rate your **happiness**? How would you have rated it ten years ago? If you continue on the path you're on, how do you suspect you'll rate it ten years from now?

- On a scale from 1 to 10, how would you rate your **sense of larger meaning and purpose**? How would you have rated it ten years ago? If you continue on the path you're on, how do you suspect you'll rate it ten years from now?

THE PRESENT

What year is it now? _____

What is your age? _____

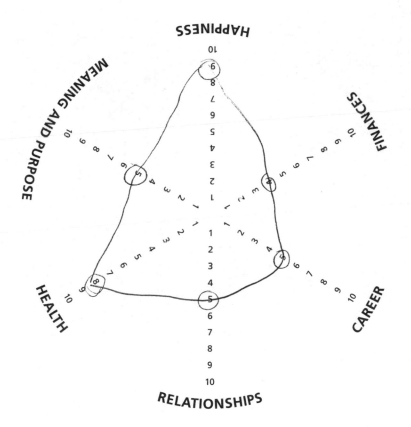

THE PAST

What year was it ten years ago? _____

What age were you then? _____

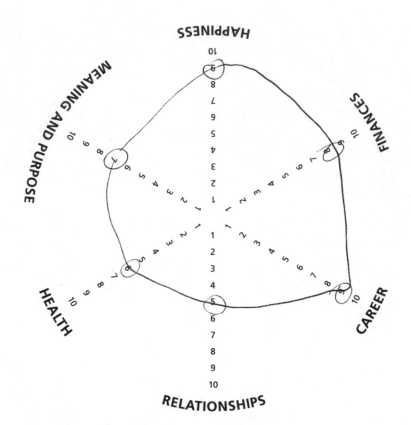

THE FUTURE

What year will it be ten years from now? _____

What age will you be then? _____

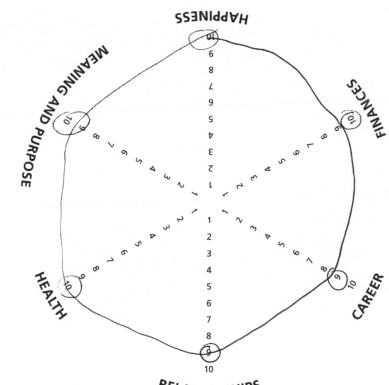

·

A FINAL THOUGHT

As we reach the end of our journey together, it may be just the beginning of a whole new life for you. While you may find you already have everything you need to succeed, you can always come back and repeat a particular technique. Having the DVD/CD/downloads is like having me on tap 24 hours a day as your own personal coach.

Here are a few things to remember before you go:

- *It isn't what you're born with or what happens to you in life, it's the choices you make along the way that determine your ultimate destiny.*
- *No matter what has happened to you up until this point in your life, you will always have choices about how you move forward.*
- *Absolutely everyone can be happy.*
- *Our goal in clearing up the limiting associations of your past is freedom – the freedom from chronic or habitual unpleasant emotions, and the freedom to live your life on your terms in pursuit of what matters most to you.*

- *When we expand the present, we have more power available to us to do whatever it is we want to do.*
- *The best way to predict the future is to create it.*

I want to let you know that I have the utmost respect for your choosing to improve yourself and the quality of your life. I think self-improvement is such a noble pursuit because it helps not only you but also the people around you, ultimately making the world a better place for all of us.

I hope we meet some day, and that your life becomes more and more wonderful in ways that you couldn't have possibly imagined before we started. I send you my blessings.

Good luck!

Paul McKenna

THE

Change Your Destiny
28-Day Journal

'Keeping a journal will absolutely change your life in ways you've never imagined.'

OPRAH WINFREY

Welcome to the Change Your Destiny 28-Day Journal

For the next 28 days, you will reinforce everything you've learned in this book by simply repeating key exercises at deliberately chosen intervals and noting down at least three things each day that are noticeably different about what happens, how you experience what happens, or what you do (or don't do) during the day.

If you have already begun to experience changes, this journal will help you to deepen them and spread them throughout your life. If you are still wondering how much of a difference reading this book and doing the exercises as I have instructed will make in your ultimate destiny, the journal will ensure that you not only experience change, but you make those changes for good.

Do not underestimate the power of positive reinforcement!

DAY 1

- Listen to the *Change Your Destiny* trance on the CD
- Listen to *Change Your World in 7 Minutes* on the CD
- Do the *Havening* exercise on the DVD

THREE NEW THINGS I'VE NOTICED ABOUT MYSELF OR MY LIFE TODAY INCLUDE...

1

_____

_____

_____

2

_____

_____

_____

3

_____

_____

_____

DAY 2

- Listen to the *Change Your Destiny* trance on the CD
- Listen to *Change Your World in 7 Minutes* on the CD
- Do the *Role Model Step In / Ultimate Self* exercise on the DVD

THREE NEW THINGS I'VE NOTICED ABOUT MYSELF OR MY LIFE TODAY INCLUDE...

1

_____

_____

_____

2

_____

_____

_____

3

_____

_____

_____

DAY 3

- Listen to the *Change Your Destiny* trance on the CD
- Listen to *Change Your World in 7 Minutes* on the CD
- Do the *Change Your Luck – Change Your Life* exercise on the DVD

THREE NEW THINGS I'VE NOTICED ABOUT MYSELF OR MY LIFE TODAY INCLUDE...

1

_____

_____

_____

2

_____

_____

_____

3

_____

_____

_____

DAY 4

- Listen to the *Change Your Destiny* trance on the CD
- Listen to *Change Your World in 7 Minutes* on the CD
- Do the *Living Your Values / Your Perfect Day* exercise on the DVD

THREE NEW THINGS I'VE NOTICED ABOUT MYSELF OR MY LIFE TODAY INCLUDE...

1

_____

_____

_____

2

_____

_____

_____

3

_____

_____

_____

DAY 5

- Listen to the *Change Your Destiny* trance on the CD
- Listen to *Change Your World in 7 Minutes* on the CD
- Do the *Life Perspective* exercise on the DVD

THREE NEW THINGS I'VE NOTICED ABOUT MYSELF OR MY LIFE TODAY INCLUDE...

1
_____

_____

_____

2
_____

_____

_____

3
_____

_____

_____

DAY 6

- Listen to the *Change Your Destiny* trance on the CD
- Listen to *Change Your World in 7 Minutes* on the CD

THREE NEW THINGS I'VE NOTICED ABOUT MYSELF OR MY LIFE TODAY INCLUDE…

1

_____

_____

_____

2

_____

_____

_____

3

_____

_____

_____

DAY 7

- Listen to the *Change Your Destiny* trance on the CD
- Listen to *Change Your World in 7 Minutes* on the CD

THREE NEW THINGS I'VE NOTICED ABOUT MYSELF OR MY LIFE TODAY INCLUDE...

1

_____

_____

_____

2

_____

_____

_____

3

_____

_____

_____

DAY 8

- Listen to the *Change Your Destiny* trance on the CD
- Listen to *Change Your World in 7 Minutes* on the CD
- Do the *Change Your Luck – Change Your Life* exercise on the DVD
- Choose any other exercise as desired

THREE NEW THINGS I'VE NOTICED ABOUT MYSELF OR MY LIFE TODAY INCLUDE...

1

_____

_____

_____

2

_____

_____

_____

3

_____

_____

_____

DAY 9

- Listen to the *Change Your Destiny* trance on the CD
- Listen to *Change Your World in 7 Minutes* on the CD
- Do the *Change Your Luck – Change Your Life* exercise on the DVD
- Choose any other exercise as desired

THREE NEW THINGS I'VE NOTICED ABOUT MYSELF OR MY LIFE TODAY INCLUDE...

1

2

3

DAY 10

- Listen to the *Change Your Destiny* trance on the CD
- Listen to *Change Your World in 7 Minutes* on the CD
- Do the *Change Your Luck – Change Your Life* exercise on the DVD
- Choose any other exercise as desired

THREE NEW THINGS I'VE NOTICED ABOUT MYSELF OR MY LIFE TODAY INCLUDE...

1

_____

_____

_____

2

_____

_____

_____

3

_____

_____

_____

DAY 11

- Listen to the *Change Your Destiny* trance on the CD
- Listen to *Change Your World in 7 Minutes* on the CD
- Do the *Change Your Luck – Change Your Life* exercise on the DVD
- Choose any other exercise as desired

THREE NEW THINGS I'VE NOTICED ABOUT MYSELF OR MY LIFE TODAY INCLUDE...

1

_____

_____

_____

2

_____

_____

_____

3

_____

_____

_____

DAY 12

- Listen to the *Change Your Destiny* trance on the CD
- Listen to *Change Your World in 7 Minutes* on the CD
- Do the *Change Your Luck – Change Your Life* exercise on the DVD
- Choose any other exercise as desired

THREE NEW THINGS I'VE NOTICED ABOUT MYSELF OR MY LIFE TODAY INCLUDE...

1

_____

_____

_____

2

_____

_____

_____

3

_____

_____

_____

DAY 13

- Listen to the *Change Your Destiny* trance on the CD
- Listen to *Change Your World in 7 Minutes* on the CD
- Do the *Change Your Luck – Change Your Life* exercise on the DVD
- Choose any other exercise as desired

THREE NEW THINGS I'VE NOTICED ABOUT MYSELF OR MY LIFE TODAY INCLUDE...

1

_____

_____

_____

2

_____

_____

_____

3

_____

_____

_____

DAY 14

- Listen to the *Change Your Destiny* trance on the CD
- Listen to *Change Your World in 7 Minutes* on the CD
- Do the *Change Your Luck – Change Your Life* exercise on the DVD
- Choose any other exercise as desired

THREE NEW THINGS I'VE NOTICED ABOUT MYSELF OR MY LIFE TODAY INCLUDE...

1

_____

_____

_____

2

_____

_____

_____

3

_____

_____

_____

DAY 15

- Listen to the *Change Your Destiny* trance on the CD
- Listen to *Change Your World in 7 Minutes* on the CD
- Do the *Change Your Luck – Change Your Life* exercise on the DVD
- Choose any other exercise as desired

THREE NEW THINGS I'VE NOTICED ABOUT MYSELF OR MY LIFE TODAY INCLUDE...

1

_____

_____

_____

2

_____

_____

_____

3

_____

_____

_____

DAY 16

- Listen to the *Change Your Destiny* trance on the CD
- Listen to *Change Your World in 7 Minutes* on the CD
- Do the *Change Your Luck – Change Your Life* exercise on the DVD
- Choose any other exercise as desired

THREE NEW THINGS I'VE NOTICED ABOUT MYSELF OR MY LIFE TODAY INCLUDE...

1

_____

_____

_____

2

_____

_____

_____

3

_____

_____

_____

DAY 17

- Listen to the *Change Your Destiny* trance on the CD
- Listen to *Change Your World in 7 Minutes* on the CD
- Do the *Change Your Luck – Change Your Life* exercise on the DVD
- Choose any other exercise as desired

THREE NEW THINGS I'VE NOTICED ABOUT MYSELF OR MY LIFE TODAY INCLUDE...

1

_____

_____

_____

2

_____

_____

_____

3

_____

_____

_____

DAY 18

- Listen to the *Change Your Destiny* trance on the CD
- Listen to *Change Your World in 7 Minutes* on the CD
- Do the *Change Your Luck – Change Your Life* exercise on the DVD
- Choose any other exercise as desired

THREE NEW THINGS I'VE NOTICED ABOUT MYSELF OR MY LIFE TODAY INCLUDE...

1

_____

_____

_____

2

_____

_____

_____

3

_____

_____

_____

DAY 19

- Listen to the *Change Your Destiny* trance on the CD
- Listen to *Change Your World in 7 Minutes* on the CD
- Do the *Change Your Luck – Change Your Life* exercise on the DVD
- Choose any other exercise as desired

THREE NEW THINGS I'VE NOTICED ABOUT MYSELF OR MY LIFE TODAY INCLUDE...

1

2

3

DAY 20

- Listen to the *Change Your Destiny* trance on the CD
- Listen to *Change Your World in 7 Minutes* on the CD
- Do the *Change Your Luck – Change Your Life* exercise on the DVD
- Choose any other exercise as desired

THREE NEW THINGS I'VE NOTICED ABOUT MYSELF OR MY LIFE TODAY INCLUDE...

1

_____

_____

_____

2

_____

_____

_____

3

_____

_____

_____

DAY 21

- Listen to the *Change Your Destiny* trance on the CD
- Listen to *Change Your World in 7 Minutes* on the CD
- Do the *Change Your Luck – Change Your Life* exercise on the DVD
- Choose any other exercise as desired

THREE NEW THINGS I'VE NOTICED ABOUT MYSELF OR MY LIFE TODAY INCLUDE...

1

2

3

DAY 22

- Listen to the *Change Your Destiny* trance on the CD
- Listen to *Change Your World in 7 Minutes* on the CD
- Choose any other exercise as desired

THREE NEW THINGS I'VE NOTICED ABOUT MYSELF OR MY LIFE TODAY INCLUDE...

1

_____

_____

_____

2

_____

_____

_____

3

_____

_____

_____

DAY 23

- Listen to the *Change Your Destiny* trance on the CD
- Listen to *Change Your World in 7 Minutes* on the CD
- Choose any other exercise as desired

THREE NEW THINGS I'VE NOTICED ABOUT MYSELF OR MY LIFE TODAY INCLUDE...

1

_____

_____

_____

2

_____

_____

_____

3

_____

_____

_____

DAY 24

- Listen to the *Change Your Destiny* trance on the CD
- Listen to *Change Your World in 7 Minutes* on the CD
- Choose any other exercise as desired

THREE NEW THINGS I'VE NOTICED ABOUT MYSELF OR MY LIFE TODAY INCLUDE...

1

_____

_____

_____

2

_____

_____

_____

3

_____

_____

_____

DAY 25

- Listen to the *Change Your Destiny* trance on the CD
- Listen to *Change Your World in 7 Minutes* on the CD
- Choose any other exercise as desired

THREE NEW THINGS I'VE NOTICED ABOUT MYSELF OR MY LIFE TODAY INCLUDE...

1

_____

_____

_____

2

_____

_____

_____

3

_____

_____

_____

DAY 26

- Listen to the *Change Your Destiny* trance on the CD
- Listen to *Change Your World in 7 Minutes* on the CD
- Choose any other exercise as desired

THREE NEW THINGS I'VE NOTICED ABOUT MYSELF OR MY LIFE TODAY INCLUDE...

1

_____

_____

_____

2

_____

_____

_____

3

_____

_____

_____

DAY 27

- Listen to the *Change Your Destiny* trance on the CD
- Listen to *Change Your World in 7 Minutes* on the CD
- Choose any other exercise as desired

THREE NEW THINGS I'VE NOTICED ABOUT MYSELF OR MY LIFE TODAY INCLUDE...

1

2

3

DAY 28

- Listen to the *Change Your Destiny* trance on the CD
- Listen to *Change Your World in 7 Minutes* on the CD
- Choose any other exercise as desired

THREE NEW THINGS I'VE NOTICED ABOUT MYSELF OR MY LIFE TODAY INCLUDE...

1

_____

_____

_____

2

_____

_____

_____

3

_____

_____

_____

THANKS

Wow – what a journey! I don't know how many books I have left to write, but as long as people want to make their lives better and have problems to solve, then I will be writing books and making products to help them.

I love all my books, but this is my favourite to date, because I believe it does the most for the reader with the least amount of effort. Although it has been an extraordinary journey, taking everything I know and refining it into a relatively simple system that creates massive positive life change on so many levels has been a challenge and a joy!

The people who have helped and supported me during this project I want to truly thank: Dr Ronald Ruden, Dr Richard Bandler, Professor Michael Carmi and Louise Carmi, Professor Richard Wiseman, Steve Crabb, Kate Davey, Mike Osborne, Doug Young, Robert Kirby, Mari Roberts, Dr George Pransky, Dr Keith Blevins, Genpo Roshi, Dr Wendy Denning, Dr Frank Nyi, Nigel Clay, Anne Jirsh, Paul Duddridge, Graham James, my wonderful parents: Joan and my late father William McKenna, John Arroyo, Robert Anton Wilson,

Deborah Thom, Sir Graeme Lamb, Neal Reading, Matthew Christian, Kevin Laye, Larry Finlay, Janine Giovanni, Tom Weldon, Alex Tuppen, Jonn Serrie, Andrew Sunnucks, Mike Stobbie, Simon Cowell, Professor Dean Radin and Emily Aspland.

Also all the people who helped in the development of this system by participating in the various studies, experiments and deconstructions of their life challenges, and embraced the possibility of a better life that made it possible to create this system.

However, a special thank you to the brilliant Michael Neill, always a joy to work with, an extraordinary person in every sense, and who is subtly relentless in getting more potential out of people than they ever dreamed they have. Thank you, my friend!